The Purpose of All Activity

A Scientific Theory of Human Behavior

Walter S. Foster

TotalRecall Publications, Inc.
1103 Middlecreek
Friendswood, Texas 77546
281-992-3131 TEL
www.totalrecallpress.com

All rights reserved, except as permitted under the United States Copyright Act of 1976. No part of this publication may be reproduced, stored in a retrieval system, or transmitted in any form or by any means electronic or mechanical or by photocopying, recording, or otherwise, without prior permission of the publisher. Exclusive worldwide content publication/distribution by TotalRecall Publications, Inc.

Copyright © 2025 by: Walter S. Foster

ISBN: 978-1-64883-266-6
UPC: 6-43977-42666-8

FIRST EDITION
1 2 3 4 5 6 7 8 9 10

The scanning, uploading and distribution of this book via the internet or via any other means without the permission of the publisher is illegal and punishable by law. Please purchase only authorized electronic editions, and do not participate in or encourage electronic piracy of copyrighted materials. Your support of the author's rights is appreciated.

Table of Contents

Introduction	IV
MOVEMENT — 1	
The three Types of Movement:	1
Cooling and Expansive Movement.	1
Dispersion and Gravitational Movement.	1
Reactions and Chemical Movement.	2
INSTINCTIVE ACTIVITY — 3	
Instinctive activity is individual movement with a direction.	3
The three types of instinctive activity	5
Individual instinctive activity and directions	7
Collective instinctive activity and norms.	8
Historical instinctive activity and direction	9
LEARNED ACTIVITY — 11	
Learned activity is instinctive activity with a collective objective	11
The four types of learned activity	11
Individual learned activity and training	12
Family learned activity and reinforcement	13
Social learned activity and specialization	14
Conceptual learned activity and objectives	15
DEVELOPED ACTIVITY — 17	
Developed Activity is learned activity with an historical purpose.	17
The four types of developed activity	17
Individual developed activity and habits.	18
Emotional developed activity and capitalism.	18
Politically developed activity and democracy	25
Historical developed activity and purpose	32
CONCLUSION	39

Introduction

If we think about our species compared to all other species there is clearly no comparison. In the past 8,000 years we have increased in number from 8 million (8,000,000) to over 8 billion (8,000,0000,000) an increase of 1,000 times. During the same period, our life expectancy has tripled from 25 years to over 75 years. From space our alterations to our environment to improve our lifestyle are infinitely greater than the alterations to our environment of any other species. The fundamental question is what has caused our dramatic success.

The cause is that we have learned to struggle for life collectively rather than individually; through collective historical knowledge rather than just through individual genetic knowledge.

This change to collective survival has occurred over several thousand years as we have learned to transmit knowledge in area after area of our life. Sexual specialization, family norms, group habits, tribal traditions, national laws and species knowledge have dramatically increased our survivability.

If we look at each of our instincts, we can see that our responses increasingly involve collective, rather than just individual, responses. For example, 8,000 years ago if we were cold, we would shiver or move into the sun. Today instead of shivering or moving into the sun we put on clothes, turn up the thermostat or go inside our house. In each case we are taking advantage of historic knowledge – of historic facts, skills, objects and behavior that increase the survivability of our species.

Similarly, 8,000 years ago if we were hungry or thirsty, we would pick berries or drink from a stream. Today, because of our collective knowledge, we turn on a faucet, open a can of soda, or open a package of cookies. We turn on a faucet, open a can of soda or a package of food only because of collective knowledge about plumbing and faucets, packaging and cooking food. 8,000 years ago, we could walk slowly and carefully in our bare feet. Today we can walk or run quickly with socks and shoes or drive a car. We choose socks, shoes and cars because they avoid pain and because it is quicker and easier.

8,000 years ago, we could scratch one another's back and touch one another to maintain a relationship. Today we officially marry and protect each other for life. 8,000 years ago, we could instinctively shelter our offspring through our physical presence. Today we send our children to school so they can learn to protect themselves. 8,000 years ago, if we were ill, we would use our immune systems to cure our illness. Today we not only use our immune system, we use antibiotics and a thousand other medicines.

8,000 years ago, if we wanted to fight, we used bows and arrows. Today if we want to fight, we use bullets and bombs. In each case our educated response is infinitely more effective than our instinctive one.

The crucial point of these behaviors, however, is that we have no choice. We are genetically programmed to select life over death – to select pleasure over pain, warmth over cold, food over hunger, water over thirst, health over sickness, easier over harder behavior and comfort over discomfort. In short, we are genetically programmed to select more functional knowledgeable behavior over less functional instinctive behavior; to select the more survivable learned collective behavior over the less survivable automatic individual behavior.

In summary, the purpose of instinctive behavior is physical survival through sensations and instincts. The purpose of learned behavior is psychological survival through reflection and experience. And the purpose of understood behavior is historical survival after death through making the world a better place to live.

The Purpose of All Activity

MOVEMENT

The three Types of Movement:

Our universe began with movement. There are three types of movement.

- Cooling and Expansive Movement.
- Dispersion and Gravitational Movement.
- Reactions and Chemical Movement.

Each type of movement develops from an earlier type of movement and all movement started with the big bang.

Cooling and Expansive Movement.

Movement in our universe began with the big bang approximately 13 billion years ago. We do not know what caused the big bang but it provided the energy behind all movement. The enormous energy released by the big bang caused all matter to expand outward from the center of our universe, the center of the big bang.

Dispersion and Gravitational Movement.

We know from Einstein that there is a direct relationship between energy and mass. According to the formula $E=MC^2$ the big bang must have created enormous amounts of mass all hurtling outward from the center of the big bang as the universe cooled. However, within that overall movement outward there were adjustments for the force of gravity within subsets of matter and their individual gravitational forces resulting from their mass.

Reactions and Chemical Movement.

At the instant of creation all the energy was in the form of hydrogen gas hurtling outward through our universe. We know from our basic chemical knowledge that the hydrogen gas is very unstable and releases energy in the forms of light and mass as it consolidates. As the energy dissipated and the universe cooled, matter consolidated and acquired gravity which increased the consolidation of all matter through reactions and chemical movements. As matter consolidated complex carbon atoms created consolidations of matter that had the capability to replicate themselves.

INSTINCTIVE ACTIVITY

Instinctive activity is individual movement with a direction.

Instinctive activity is determined by our genes. The purpose of all instinctive activity is survival. The challenge is that animal survival is different from human survival. The purpose of all animal activity has changed from survival after death through genetic reproduction to human activity where survival after death occurs through knowledge transmission. Survival has changed for humans from survival after death through increasing the number of an animal's species in a natural environment to increasing the dominance of the human species in an historical environment. It has changed from self-interest in a natural world to enlightened self-interest in a human world.

The clarification of this purpose to survive for humans has been the aim of philosophers for centuries.

What is the purpose of all activity?

> "If there is some end (purpose) in the things we do, which we desire for its own sake, clearly this must be the chief good. Knowing this will have a great influence on how we live our lives."
> **--Aristotle, Ethics**

Aristotle was right in clarifying the most important of all questions – what the purpose of all activity is. If we know the purpose of all activity, we can prioritize our behavior to best achieve that purpose. Because of a lack of scientific knowledge, Aristotle attempted to answer the question philosophically. He came up with the answer that the purpose of all activity is great deeds by great men.

Many individuals have now settled on a more universal purpose of all activity:

> "Personally, and professionally, I am motivated by the desire to leave the world a better place."
> --**Jami Dimon, Chairman and Chief /Executive Officer, JPMorgan Chase, Letter to Shareholders, 2021 Annual Report, Page 2**

This latter definition would suggest that the purpose of all activity is to survive through historical survival, i.e. through contributions *to making the world a better place.*

This purpose of instinctive activity – physical survival -- is determined by our genes because all our genes have been selected because they contribute to our individual *physical survival.* This theory suggests we are programmed to shape those individual unconscious instinctive reactions to survive into a collective *historical* conduct *to survive.*

Therefore, while the fundamental force **increasing animal survival** is the **natural selection of individual genes**, the fundamental force **increasing human survival** is the **historical selection of collective knowledge** – the historical selection of "facts, skills, objects and behavior" that increase the dominance i.e. the survival of our species. **Our contribution to that knowledge, however small, permits us to survive historically after our death through those contributions.**

The three types of instinctive activity

Instinctive activity is individual movement with a direction – a unique course along which each of us moves to survive physically. However, this direction, because it is unique for each of us, is admittedly hard to clarify. Each human of the eight billion inhabitants on this earth has a different way to achieve survival. For many it is a struggle for survival through raising their children who are healthier, wealthier, better educated and more mature and wiser than they are. For others, it is a struggle for survival, as well, through making our friends, our company or our country more productive, prosperous, fair and just. And for others it is a struggle for survival, as well, through contributing to knowledge that increases our collective survival through science and art. The result is that for each individual his/her specific purpose for survival is unique. It consists of contributions to his/her children, family, friends, job, country and/or environment that make the world a better place for humans.

For example, for our species to survive, both females and males must survive. *In quite simple terms,* we can see that they survive in two complimentary but different ways. Biologically, women survive though their genes and through nurturing and protecting offspring. Similarly, men survive biologically through their genes, competition, and impregnating females. Psychologically, the female approach to survival leads to empathy, equality, political democracy, beauty and for empathizing with and caring for children as well as the weaker and less fortunate. Similarly, psychologically, the masculine approach to survival leads to productivity, hierarchy, economic capitalism, and truth and respect for the most able and productive.

Our challenge, at the individual level, is that we lack self-knowledge. Our challenge is that we tend to over identify with one or the other approaches to survival depending upon our capabilities and genes. *In very simple terms*, if we are best at sensual knowledge -- nurturing, empathy, and beauty -- we value equality, democracy, and individual rights most highly. *"In very simple terms,"* if we are best at motor knowledge -- productivity, competence, and truth -- we value hierarchy, capitalism, and responsibility most highly. However, if our strength is motor knowledge, only by understanding and valuing the contributions of others and their sensual knowledge can we successfully contribute to those with sensual knowledge. And vice versa. If our strength is sensual knowledge, only by understanding and valuing the contributions of others and their motor knowledge can we successfully contribute to others.

Individual instinctive activity and directions

The question is how did this struggle for self-knowledge evolve and develop. It evolved through our basic struggle for survival though physical instincts directing us to survive including:

- Our instincts for **survival** through **oxygen**. When we are drowning, we must move towards air, or we will die.
- Our instincts for **survival** through **water**. When we are thirsty, we must move towards water, or we will die.
- Our instincts for **survival** through **food**. When we are starving, we must move towards food, or we will die.
- Our instincts for **survival** through **warmth**. When we are cold, we must move towards warmth, or we will die.
- Our instincts for **survival** through the **avoidance of pain**. When we are in pain, we must move away from pain, or we will die.
- Finally, our instincts for **survival** through **sexual reproduction**. When we are attracted to the opposite sex, we must move toward sexual intercourse or we will die genetically.

In each case, our sensual and motor nervous systems react immediately whenever there is a threat of harm. This direct struggle for physical survival is automatic. When we are without oxygen, we never think we must survive so we must breathe. We breathe automatically. Our responses to our other needs are also automatic. And our overwhelming instinct to survive is so great we never even think about it.

Collective instinctive activity and norms.

If we think about our species compared to all other species however, there is clearly no comparison. In the past 8,000 years we have increased in number from 8 million (8,000,000) to over 8 billion (8,000,0000,000) an increase of 1,000 times. During the same period, our life expectancy has tripled form 25 years to over 75 years. From space our alterations to our environment to improve our lifestyle are infinitely greater than the alterations to our environment of any other species. While it is in our nature to always complain about our inefficiencies, it is important to remember that our species has learned to prosper despite plagues, world wars, epidemics, climate changes, pestilence, etc., etc., etc. After such a successful history how can we not overcome the remaining minor shortcomings that we face today. While some may suggest that this is an optimistic view of human nature, our success has nothing to do with optimism or pessimism but rather our genetic imperative to survive. This genetic imperative does not mean we will survive without struggle. It merely means that in the long run we have no choice but to select functional behavior over dysfunctional behavior and survival over death. It does not mean we will avoid wars, pandemics, climate mistakes etc. merely that when the harm becomes great enough and clear enough, we will stop fighting and dysfunctional behavior and devote sufficient energy to developing more functional behavior that increases the dominance of our species.

Furthermore, there is the fundamental problem of ignorance. If knowledge consists of functional "facts, skills, objects and behavior" ignorance consists of a lack of knowledge, a lack of "facts, skills objects and behavior" or dysfunctional "facts, skills, objects and behavior." Much of a society's energy has to be devoted to inspiring, rewarding and clarifying functional "facts, skills, objects and behavior" and negatively reinforcing dysfunctional "facts, skill, objects and behavior." As "knowledge" explodes in complexity the challenge for governments and cultures is to be equally creative in developing laws, custom, regulations and educational systems that are equally as complex and functional as the challenges they are trying to overcome. Our genetic imperative to survive has developed over centuries and led us to expand our purpose for living to include historical survival.

Historical instinctive activity and direction

Our genetic imperative to survive has developed over centuries and led us to expand our purpose for living to include historical survival.

In contrast, natural survival for all other animals focuses only on health, reproduction, and individual physical survival. Because animals have no conscious history, they have no way to make their environment better for future generations through species knowledge. In contrast humans have a history that has dramatically expanded our functional "facts, skills, objects and behavior" and reduced our dysfunctional "facts, skills, objects and behavior" through the efforts of previous generations. These efforts reinforce us to change our focus to functional behavior that benefits not just oneself but benefits our entire species as well and discourages dysfunctional "facts, skills, objects and behavior" that benefits only oneself at the expense of the rest of our species.

The reason this enlightened self-interest for future survival is more satisfying than all our other efforts to gain satisfaction is because these lesser forms of self-interest end with our death. In contrast, enlightened self-interest permits us to live after our death. After we have achieved personal **pleasure**, family **joy**, and social **happiness** we are genetically programmed to become bored and strive for the historical **contentment** that comes from meaningful and purposeful conduct. It is this objective for meaningful and purposeful conduct that leads to progress i.e., *the increased dominance of our species through functional knowledge.*

LEARNED ACTIVITY

Learned activity is instinctive activity with a collective objective

Learned objectives direct us how to strive for survival as part of a family, a part of a society and a part of a culture. Our personal experience, families, jobs, cultures and environments constantly reinforce us to gain functional knowledge that increases our ability and desire to survive. Because of our increased historical knowledge, external capacities and improved physical, cultural and historical environments, we have dramatically increased our capacity and desire to survive.

The four types of learned activity

The four types of learned activity are
- individual learned activity and training,
- family learned activity and reinforcement,
- social learned activity and specialization and
- conceptual learned activity and **objectives**.

Genes determine our individual learned activity that
- trains our individual activity in our physical environment.
- reinforces our social activity in our family environment

- specializes our economic activity in our political environment. And;
- educates our historical activity in our contemporary environment.

Individual learned activity and training

Our genes **indirectly** determine our conscious struggle for survival through learned activity.

- *Genes* **indirectly** determine learned **capacities** that increase our ability to survive by walking, running, and swimming, etc.
- *Genes* also indirectly determine learned **sensations** that increase our desire to survive by avoiding thirst, cold, hunger, fear, and pain and obtaining sexual satisfaction.
- *Genes* also indirectly determine learned **thoughts** that increase our capability to survive by learning how to use calculators, telescopes, computers, cell phones etc.
- *Genes* also indirectly determine learned **feelings** that increase our determination to survive through feelings of warmth, comfort, pleasure, joy, happiness, contentment and sexual arousal.

Therefore, genes **indirectly** determine all our learned behavior as well as directly determining our instinctive behavior. These genetic instincts determine learned behavior that supports:

- our struggle for individual survival in our **physical environment.**
- our struggle for social survival in our **family environment.**
- our struggle for economic survival in our **political environment.** And:
- our struggle for historical survival in our **contemporary environment.**

Family learned activity and reinforcement

Our behavioral learning also develops through our instincts for family survival including:

- Our instincts for family survival through **attention.** When we are a baby, we must obtain family attention when we are hungry, or we will die.
- Our instincts for family survival through **affection.** When we are ignored, we must move to obtain family affection, or we will die.
- Our instincts for family survival through **protection.** When we are afraid, we must move to obtain family protection, or we will die.
- Our instincts for family survival through the **avoidance of rejection.** When we are rejected, we must move to avoid family rejection, or we will die. And
- Finally, our instincts for family survival **through reproduction.** When we are sexually aroused, we must move to achieve reproduction of our **genes** or they will die out.

In each case, our instincts for family survival determine our learned family behavior that reduces threats to our well-being. Again, we never think we need to obtain attention to survive therefore I will cry or act out. We simply cry when we are hungry and act out when we need more attention.

Social learned activity and specialization

The next phase of learning develops through our instincts for social purpose through specialized economic and political learned behavior including:

- Learned social behavior that permits us to **fit into our** family.
- Learned economic behavior that permits us to get **a job** to make money. And,
- Learned political behavior that develops **a value system** that makes us want to work.

Each of these family adjustments, jobs and value systems is different as each of us attempts to provide behavior that increases the dominance of our species through millions of different family roles, jobs and value systems. As our knowledge exploded so did our different types of family roles, jobs and value systems.

Conceptual learned activity and objectives

The final phase of learning develops our instinctive struggle for historical behavior and objectives. The earliest example of this struggle for historical behavior through objectives was in Egypt where the attempt was made to physically survive after death through mummification and pyramids. Grave robbers and the enormity of earlier efforts to build pyramids showed these efforts to be of limited success.

A second example of our struggle for historical behavior through objectives was in Greece where an attempt was made by great and powerful military leaders to survive after death through great victories. However, even great victories, such as those of Alexander the Great, were shown to have limited success. As our environment changed it reduced the need for war heroes.

Our third example of our struggle for historical behavior through objectives was through religions which offered the opportunity to survive after death spiritually in a heaven through good behavior during our life. Again, science has offered little evidence to suggest these religious efforts have achieved any success in proving there is a heaven.

What we are left with is only one way to obtain historical survival and it is through behavior *"**that leaves the world a better place.**"* This "historical behavior" through functional objectives occurs through our contributions to our family, our friends, our nation and to anything we do that increases the dominance of our species. And the increased dominance of our species comes from historical selection of knowledge that "makes the world a better place for humans".

DEVELOPED ACTIVITY

Developed Activity is learned activity with an historical purpose.

Developed activity is learned activity with the historical purpose of increasing the dominance of our species. The purpose of developed activity as an individual, a member of a family or group, of a country and of a historical moment is to make the earth a better place for humans. It is activity whose aim is to make the world a better place for others even if it is at our expense i.e. helps others more than it helps us. It is altruistic activity whose goal is to help others even if it harms us.

The four types of developed activity

Human progress occurs because *historical selection* acts as an extension of *natural selection* by selecting functional collective knowledge, i.e., functional "facts, skills, objects and behavior" that increase collective human survival through abilities and/or feelings. **Abilities** are transmitted through *historically developed environments* that clarify how to make each individual life more purposeful through understood logical activity. **Feelings** are transmitted through *historically developed individual rights* that clarify how to make each individual life more meaningful through understood emotional activity. These functional acquired characteristics are transmitted by families, friends, cultures and nations through example, instruction, education, laws, traditions i.e., though" knowledge". It is the transmission of functional knowledge and discouragement of dysfunctional knowledge that lives on generation after generation and gives our life a meaning and purpose.

Individual developed activity and habits.

Our individual progress develops sub-consciously through habits, norms and customs that make us feel comfortable through interaction with others. These habits, norms and customs consist of thousands of subconscious interactions that make our relationships more functional and pleasant.

Emotional developed activity and capitalism.

However, while our genes program us to survive, there are an infinite number of obstacles hindering our success. These obstacles decrease our capacity to survive through fear, fatigue and ignorance and decrease our desire to survive through anger, rage and shame and they cause us to engage in dysfunctional behavior.

Most writers refer to functional and dysfunctional behavior as "good" and "bad", "moral" or "immoral", "evil" or "kind" behavior. We know now that behavior is more complicated than that. Rather than being simple black or white or good or bad, all behavior is various shades of gray, self-interested and enlightened self-interested behavior. By referring to behavior as functional and dysfunctional, the ultimate objective of collective survival is included in the word and the gradations of successful and unsuccessful behavior become clearer. Occasionally there is behavior that is overwhelmingly dysfunctional like terrorism or overwhelmingly functional like scientific discoveries of vaccinations. But in general, our behavior is a mix of dysfunctional self-interest and functional enlightened self-interest and that is what makes life so interesting and challenging.

Self-knowledge permits us to overcome our shortcomings and accept our most functional way to maximize the passion and purpose of our capabilities and apply them in the most functional manner to make the world a better place. For most of us our most functional form of contribution is through our children. However, instead of just helping them to survive physically, our struggle is to help them to survive psychologically. Our objective is to help them survive in an increasingly complex world through love and education that can help them pass their version of passion and purpose on to their own children and grandchildren, and to their community and country as well. This passion and purpose to develop a meaningful and purposeful life is the essence of the struggle for life after death for it provides the emotional and intellectual resources to maximize our contributions that live on after our death.

As a result, every individual in a democratic nation has the capacity to have a meaningful and purposeful life. By being given the right to choose our activity we are all given the opportunity to engage in the most functional behavior (or the least dysfunctional behavior) that we are capable of in making the world a better place.

In each case we must first satisfy our physical needs before we progress to satisfying our social needs; our social needs before we satisfy our economic needs and our economic needs before we can satisfy our historical needs. The result is that while our ultimate aim is to make the world a better place and to obtain historical survival, the majority of our time and for some individuals, all of their time is spent trying to satisfy their own physical, social and economic needs.

While we think of knowledge as complex, our personal knowledge includes the most mundane of insights and judgments about our abilities and feelings. These abilities and feelings are unique to each individual whether they are about our learning to walk, attract a mate, understand our environment, make friends, or find a job – literally thousands of abilities and feelings that determine who we are as an individual. And this capacity to develop unique abilities and feelings and to develop them in a way that most increases our collective survival has resulted in humans as the most successful of all species.

Just as we face a constant physical tension between males and females, we face a constant social tension between democracy and capitalism. The challenge for each of us individually and each nation collectively is to develop not only by valuing the capabilities where we are most competent but also by understanding and respecting the opposite capabilities. The challenge is to develop constitutional checks and balances to protect us from too much capitalism and too little democracy or too much democracy with too little capitalism. Our challenge is to cooperate with one another rather than to fight one another. If we are best at nurturing and affection and believe in freedom and democracy, our challenge is to recognize our biases and learn to respect competitiveness, competence, and capitalism. If we are best at competitiveness and competence and believe in responsibility and capitalism, our challenge is to recognize our biases and to learn to admire nurturing, affection, and democracy. What our families, nations, and principles need to do is educate tolerance and negatively reinforce beliefs that we have the only true way to heaven and/or to right and wrong.

There are two types of struggles for individual knowledge that lead to the increased dominance of our species. The first is based on motor knowledge that increases our capacity to survive. The second is based on sensual knowledge that increases our desire to survive.
We cannot survive physically without cooperation between females and males. Similarly, we cannot survive socially and historically without cooperation between democracy and capitalism. Therefore, our challenge is to function as smoothly as we can within a democratic political system and a capitalist economic system. As

unpopular as it may be, successful nations must educate and reinforce their citizens to recognize the legitimacy of soft political and aesthetic knowledge as well as hard economic and scientific knowledge and vice versa. They educate and reinforce their citizens to recognize that while we are equal in terms of our political rights, we are unequal in terms of our economic capabilities. Nations can only accomplish this objective once they have developed and transmitted the necessary social cooperative knowledge to minimize the effects of our biological egotistical knowledge. Nations can only accomplish this objective when they have developed their citizen's individual needs and drives into collective meaning and purpose. This is an unending and all-consuming process. And historical progress comes from the corrective learning resulting from the negative reinforcement of dysfunctional behavior as well as the encouragement resulting from positive reinforcement of functional behavior.

Struggles for knowledge				
Struggles for Knowledge	Capacities and Physical Movement Through	Sensations and Physical Warmth Through	Abilities and Mental Movement Through	Feelings and Mental Warmth Through
Types of Knowledge	Ships Cars Highways Airplanes Rockets	Clothes Buildings Houses Furnaces Conditioners	Calculators Telescopes Computers Cell Phones Science	Marriage Specialization Norms, Laws Affection Aesthetics
Types of Knowledge	Physical Motor Knowledge	Physical Sensual Knowledge	Mental Motor Knowledge	Mental Sensual Knowledge
That are The Result of	Motor Instruction	Sensual Instruction	Motor Education	Sensual Education

- Our ability to survive has increased enormously through our increased ability to move. From ships to bikes to trains, to cars, to airplanes and to rockets we have made enormous increases through objects in the ease and speed with which we can move physically to satisfy our needs.
- Our desire to survive has increased enormously though our ability to control our environment through objects to obtain warmth, remain cool and obtain food. From clothes, houses, buildings, furnaces, air conditioners and farms we have made increases in our ability to control the physical temperature and humidity of our environments to make us feel comfortable and to provide food.
- Our ability to survive has increased enormously

through our increased ability to think through education. From calculators, telescopes, computers, cell phones and science we have made enormous increases in the ease and speed with which we can communicate, analyze, calculate, think, and work collectively.
- Finally, our desire to survive has increased dramatically through our ability to feel through empathy, education, monogamous married relations, occupational specialization and aesthetics and the capacity to appreciate the contributions of others. Similarly, our capacity to survive has increased through our ability to work collectively and to negatively reinforce dysfunctional behavior like murder, crime and cruelty.

The struggle for increased need for physical movement began with the development of bikes on the ground and progressed to the development of rockets for space. The struggle for increased sensual control of our physical temperature began with clothes and progressed to air conditioners. The struggle for increased motor control of mental movement began with calculators and progressed to cell phones and science. The struggle for increased empathy began with marriage, specialization within the family and progressed to the specialization of jobs and occupations within the nation and a sense of enlightened self- interest. The key point is that reinforcement of behavior results unconsciously into the utilization of knowledge to increase collective survival indirectly as well as directly.

Sensual struggles for progress through increased individual rights are less transparent than motor struggles and take longer to be accepted. Nonetheless, sensual struggles through increased personal rights have dramatically increased the opportunity for more citizens to contribute to the dominance of our species. And no matter how small these contributions may be—living longer, obtaining better education than our parents, being healthier, raising better educated children, having a happier marriage, punishing dysfunctional behavior etc., etc., etc. Collectively, overtime, these changes dramatically affect human behavior.

Politically developed activity and democracy

Date	1700's	1800's	1900's	2000's
Types of Rights	Political rights to obtain representation	Human rights to eliminate slavery	Civil rights to vote	Women's rights to choose
Agents of Change	War	War	Laws & Demonstrations	Laws & Demonstrations
Key Events	Independence	Abolition of Slavery	Equal Education	Legal right to abortion

- The most important U.S. struggle for collective sensual knowledge during the 1700's was the struggle for **political rights**. The struggle against

Great Britain for no taxation without representation.
- The most important U.S. struggle for collective sensual knowledge during the 1800's was the struggle for **human rights**. The struggle of the North against the South for the end of slavery.
- The most important U.S. struggle for collective sensual knowledge during the 1900's was the struggle for **civil rights**. The struggle of blacks against whites for civil rights including the right to vote.
- The most important U.S. struggle for collective sensual knowledge during the 2000's is the struggle for **women's rights**. The struggle for a women's right to choose.

The struggle for progress through collective political knowledge began with Lexington and Concord and resulted in the revolutionary war. The struggle for progress through collective political knowledge began with the cessation of the South from the Union and resulted in the Civil War. The struggle for progress through collective racial knowledge began with Brown v. the Board of Education and resulted in the Civil Rights Act. The struggle for progress through collective women's knowledge began with Roe v. Wade and will result in a law that gives every woman the sole right to decide whether to have a baby.

At first glance, it looks unrealistic to expect people will choose painful, uncomfortable and/or disruptive behavior that will make the quality of life better for others in the future at the expense of their own immediate gratification. We have learned, however, by acting collectively we can modify behavior through instruction, education, and environmental structures such as laws and norms. We have learned, however, by acting collectively we can negatively reinforce dysfunctional behavior through fines, laws and prisons.

A successful example of our collective attempts to negatively reinforce dysfunctional behavior occurred with cigarette smoking. When the scientific evidence became overwhelming that cigarette smoking was a leading cause of lung cancer and a liability to the national health system, opinions about cigarette smoking changed. Individuals and governments successfully sued cigarette companies, limited access to cigarettes by minors, increased their cost through taxes and reduced cigarette advertising. The result was a substantial reduction in smoking even though the individual nicotine kick was immediate and the resulting possibility of cancer decades in the future. The important point to remember is that the U.S. accomplished this reduction in cigarette smoking and lung cancer within a democratic and capitalistic framework. It never denied U.S. citizens the choice to smoke; it merely positively and negatively reinforced individuals for their choice. It positively reinforced citizens through social pressure and education for not smoking. In addition, it negatively reinforced individuals by making cigarettes more expensive, by prohibiting the sale of cigarettes to minors, by limiting cigarette advertising, by prohibiting smoking in non-smoking areas, by prosecuting those who spread false information downplaying the dangers of smoking and by suing cigarette companies for the extra costs smoking caused the health care system.

Similarly, we are equally successful in developing functional norms, laws, rewards, and education to develop enlightened self-interested behavior that benefits others. We can reinforce functional behavior through encouragement, instruction, education, economic incentives, and free choice. Similarly, we can negatively reinforce dysfunctional behavior through taxes, laws, legislation and education.

Our struggle for historical survival through family, social, and historical knowledge provides a meaning and purpose in our life. Meaning and purpose from understanding refocuses human energies from an individual struggle for survival through our own self-interest into a collective struggle for survival through enlightened self-interest. This enlightened self-interest focuses our energy on progress for others as well as ourselves and is reinforced by collective negative as well as collective positive reinforcement.

In many cases that effort to obtain historical survival can take many years and often be unrecognized, such as a mother's willingness to sacrifice her own life both physically and psychologically for the well-being of her children and grandchildren. This maternal/familial self-sacrifice is, of course, merely an extension of the *natural struggle* for physical survival.   Hoverer there are many other examples of individuals willing to sacrifice their own life for the betterment of non-family members including their friends, company associates, and/or countrymen.

Ultimately, this struggle between sensual and motor knowledge develops egotistical behavior into cooperative behavior and cooperative behavior into contributive conduct. *Ultimately, it develops the struggle for biological survival and irresponsible reproduction into the struggle for psychological survival and responsible parenting.* We can see the enormous cost of failure to develop an empathetic and educated electorate in undeveloped nations. In these nations, there is poverty, economic corruption, and negative per capita GDP growth. In these nations, instead of just contested elections and different views, there is political unrest, social and religious violence, and civil wars.

The constant struggle for individual knowledge is self-evident. Science has clearly demonstrated the way to a healthier population through nutrition, vaccinations, hospitals, and exercise. The need for better and more effective ways to move, remain comfortable, think, and have sex are unending. They are progressing at an enormous rate through personal, social, and historical i.e., human selection.

On the other hand, collective knowledge is much slower and more difficult to transmit from generation to generation since it varies from family to family and nation to nation. For example, collective knowledge in relations between the sexes has resulted in the reduction of conflict through marriage – one female per male. Historical collective knowledge about relations between families has resulted in the reduction in conflict through laws providing principles for sharing cooperatively between groups through taxes on the wealthy and welfare for the poor. And historical progress in relations between the sexes has resulted in the reduction of conflicts through changes in customs allowing increasing freedoms of choice for women.

Like all basic struggles, the struggle for women's rights is a struggle based on the deficiency of our evolved individual genes to live in a developed collective environment. Our genes provide a concept of self-interest based on natural selection of the physically fittest male and female genes -- males through competition for females and females for attracting males. In our collective specialized economies what we need instead is a self-interest based on the historical selection of the most contributive behavior -- behavior that most increases the dominance of our species but also that maximizes our personal and social survival. What this requires is the development and education of an enlightened historical self-interest as opposed to an individual egotistical self-interest. As outlined in the previous section, what is required is the norms, customs, laws, tax incentives and recognition of contributions to knowledge that make the world a better place for our species. This selection process has increased in stages through different changes to our relationship with the opposite sex.

As mentioned in the previous chapter the most successful example of collective attempts to reduce dysfunctional behavior occurred with cigarette smoking. When scientific evidence became overwhelming that cigarette smoking was a leading cause of lung cancer and a liability to the national health system, opinions about cigarette smoking changed. Similarly, when scientific evidence became overwhelming that gender inequality reduces global productivity and well-being, opinions about gender inequality changed. Individuals and states are already successfully suing individuals and companies that are discriminating against or harassing women, increasing the cost of gender prejudice. The result has been a substantial reduction in gender prejudice even though the individual opportunity to harass women remains and the possibility of a successful lawsuit for discriminating is small.

The important point to remember is that the U.S. can accomplish this reduction in gender discrimination within a democratic and capitalistic framework. It need not deny U.S. citizens the right to discriminate; it can merely positively and negatively reinforce individuals for their choice. It can positively reinforce citizens through social pressure and education for encouraging gender equality.

In addition, it can negatively reinforce individuals by taking them to court for sexual harassment and discrimination. By teaching gender respect in schools, by encouraging entertainment heroes to include those who respect women, by prohibiting sexual harassment in the workplace, by prosecuting and exposing those who actively try to restrict a woman's choice, we can reduce our natural genetic gender bias.

Historical developed activity and purpose

Men, as supposed losers in any reduction of gender bias, are in fact equal beneficiaries in getting rid of gender discrimination. Prejudice, getting something unfairly, undermines the confidence of the recipient as well as the abused and is demoralizing. While men naturally feel superior to women as children because of their greater physical size and strength, this apparent advantage in our modern society disappears with age and education. Clearly in today's technological world a woman flying an F-17 can be equally as powerful as a man. This is particularly clear from an historical perspective in other areas as well.
No one in his right mind would suggest today that we should be ruled by Great Britain. While it appears today that the United States was the winner of the Revolutionary War, with historical hindsight, it is obvious that Great Britain was also the winner. Only a strong and independent United States could have saved Great Britain from Nazi Germany during World War II. A strong United States resulted in the purposeful and meaningful

behavior that enhances the survival of democracy and reduces totalitarianism.

Similarly, no one in his right mind would suggest today that the South should be allowed to have slaves. While it appears today that the North was the winner of the Civil War, with historical hindsight it is obvious that the South was also the winner. Only a slavery free South could become the moral, ethical, and political society that makes it part of the world's strongest and most democratic country. A slave free South resulted in the purposeful & meaningful behavior that expands the right in the Declaration of Independence that all men are created equal.

Similarly, no one in his right mind would suggest today that minorities should be denied civil rights. While it appears today that minorities were the winner of the Civil Rights Act, with historical hindsight it is obvious that the U.S. non-minorities were also the winner. Only a democratic capitalist society could have educated a productive minority work force that makes it part of the world's most prosperous country. Only a democratic and capitalist society could result in the opportunity for purposeful & meaningful behavior that can guarantee civil rights to everyone.

50 years from now it will be viewed as outrageous to suggest men should be the deciders of whether a woman should have a child. While it appears today that women were the winner in Roe v. Wade, historically it will become apparent that men are also the winners. Therefore, men need to support the struggle for women's rights as much as women because "an injustice anywhere is an injustice everywhere." Gender prejudice is as harmful to those who discriminate without being negatively reinforced as it is to those who are the recipient of the discrimination.

Only an egalitarian relationship that gives women the right to choose whether to have a child can develop the loving sexual relationship that makes men as well as women happy and productive. Only an equalitarian relationship that gives a woman the right to choose can result in the purposeful & meaningful behavior that results in progress and mature, happy marriages.

While there is general agreement that it is all right to take our life when we have a terminal physical illness, it is the general view that it is not all right to take our life to reduce our mental pain through suicide when we have a terminal mental illness—when we can no longer contribute to making the world a better place. For example, most states outlaw suicide.

If the purpose of all activity for humans is to leave the world a better place, the final question therefore is at what point is the world a better place without us. In a world of rapidly increasing medical knowledge, at what point are our emotional and financial contributions less than our emotional and financial costs.

Insurance companies for example provide a very specific description of when we are not long able to contribute to making the world a better place without the help of others. They define the 10 activities of daily living as:

- Toileting
- Bathing
- Eating
- Personal hygiene
- Grooming
- Dressing
- transferring
- Mobility
- Urinary incontinence
- Teeth brushing and grooming

In some cases, the costs of our daily living are greater than our benefits for or ability to make the world a better place for others.

On the other hand, the number of ways we can contribute to making the world a better place is almost infinite.

- With regard to our children—making our children better educated, happier, healthier and wiser than we are
- With regard to our family wives and friends by helping them be happier and more joyful.
- With regard to our jobs by making our environment better for humans.

The most important fact to remember is that preparing for a functional death must be done well ahead – preferably 2-3 years before there is a reasonable chance of dying and certainly by our early 80's. The reason preparation must be done in advance is that when we are stricken with illness or injury, we normally will be in no position to execute a decision as important as to whether or not our most functional choice is to commit suicide. In addition, unless you have read and re-read a book like "Final Exit 20/20" by Derek Humphry you probably have little or no idea of how complicated suicide is.

In my own case, for twenty years I had informed my doctors that there might be conditions that would occur in which I would not want to live. In that case, although I knew the doctors could not help me take my own life, they were at least made aware that this was my wish about my own life and not because of someone else's fault or influence.

However, at 86, everything suddenly went wrong. I had a pulmonary embolism shortly after which I had a fall which left me with 5 compression fractures in my lower back. For the first two months I was in so much pain I frequently considered suicide because no doctor would provide me more than 7 days of pain pills. After two cytoplastic procedures, the pain was reduced to a bearable level and I finally wanted once again to get up again in the morning.

Unfortunately, in the process I was not able to be a good camper and I put my wife through hell. My wife was fantastic but in spite of my best efforts I could not help but being an enormous burden.

The lessons I learned from this experience is that I must never again get in a position where someone else is determining the level of pain I have to endure. And fortunately, with no little difficulty I have now accumulated enough pain pills so that I can make my own choice to decide whether I want to live or die. I accumulated the pills by asking doctors for them when the pain became bearable and I could get by with just extra strength Tylenol. However, like most people when I tried to prepare in detail how to take my life, I found I had totally misunderstood how to ensure how to have a painless death. Again, with the help of Final Exit 20/20 I am now trying to develop the method I would like to choose to end my life. This is not an easy process and makes me realize how totally inadequate were my earlier plans for self-deliverance were. I have now decided on a mixture of drugs like Seconal and Nembutal.

Unfortunately, my clock is ticking and my remaining time when I can help making this world a better place is short. A fall, an illness, another year or two of aging and I will have to face the grim reaper. I can only say when the time comes, I am ready. I have had what seems to me a far better life than I deserve. I have been married to two incredible women who have made my life meaningful and joyful and I can never acknowledge sufficiently their support. With out my late wife Virginia and my current wife Elizabeth, I would surely have died long ago and/or lived in a cave somewhere twiddling my thumbs. All I was and could ever hope to be I owe to them. They have been the sun, the moon and the stars of my life. In short, I can never repay all I owe them and the best I can to is leave without being too big a burden.

What will probably be the greatest factor leading me to commit suicide will not be the pain or discomfort due to the gradual realization of the enormous burden I am putting on others. In spite of their protestation of how much they want me to live, the burden I will be placing on my caregivers is greater than the help I can give in return. The toll on the caregivers is often far greater than the toll on the patient and the resolution will probably take many difficult hours of thought and discussion.

CONCLUSION

In summary, the end of all activity is survival through progressive understood activity i.e., activity designed "to leave the world a better place.' The struggle for individual survival, through genes in animals, has been largely replaced by the struggle for collective survival though *understood activity* in humans. The purpose of understood activity is to make the world a better place. Therefore, while the fundamental force **shaping animal survival** is the natural selection of genes, the fundamental force **shaping human survival** is the historical selection of understood activity.

Using this approach refocuses the discussion of knowledge from observable historical "facts, skills and objects" to include feelings about personal and social "facts skills and objects." Since everyone is different, everyone will have different personal and social knowledge and a different way to contribute to making the world a better place. As a result, the most important aspect of democracy is the right for everyone to choose the behavior that is most satisfying to the individual while at the same time the most functional (or least dysfunctional) for every one else.

Corporate, Bank and Derivative Credit Risk Judgement

W. S. Foster Associates
Credit Development Specialists

W. S. Foster, President

Conducts seminars in Corporate and Bank Credit Risk Judgment.
Conducts seminars in Derivative Credit Risk Judgment and Management.
Conducts seminars in Credit Portfolio Risk Management
Conducts seminars in Evaluating Distressed Debt

W. S. Foster Associates

For over twenty years. W. S. Foster Associates has provided quality in-house training programs to a wide variety of U.S. and international institutions. The courses are for entry level as well as experienced investment bankers and financial professionals. W. S. Foster Associates' role as seminar leader has greatly enhanced the judgment and analytical skills of participants from hanks, investment hanks and rating agencies. Clients include:

Standard & Poor \s
Fannie Mae
National Australia Bank
Credit Suisse First Boston
Federal Reserve Bank of NY
Merrill Lynch
Bank of England

Jack Foster, primary instructor of W. S. Foster Associates, has unique qualifications to design and lead credit seminars. Over the past 20 years, he has conducted over 200 week long Corporate and Bank Credit Rating Seminars in over 15 countries including Saudi Arabia, Egypt, I long Kong, China, South Korea, Japan, Singapore, Indonesia, Australia, Mexico, Sweden, Switzerland, Germany, England, France, and the U.S. He started and was Chairman of the Rating Committee at JP Morgan for five years and served at JP Morgan for 20 years (1974-1994). He was the primary instructor for Standard and Poor's internal and external Bank and Corporate Credit analysis Seminars for eight years (1995-2003). He is a graduate of Williams College and the Harvard Business School.

WALTER S. (JACK) FOSTER

EMPLOYMENT

2002-2016 NEW YORK INSTITUTE OF FINANCE:
Conducted seminars in Corporate, Bank and Derivative Credit Risk Judgment in New York,
Riyadh, Chicago and San Diego
Conducted seminars in Basel III and Systemically Important Financial Institutions
Developed electronic credit and corporate finance courses

Member RMA (Risk Management Association) CMCAS (Capital Markets Credit
lysts Society and, FIAS (Fixed Income Analysts Society).

1995-2002 TANDARD AND POOR'S:
Primary instructor for internal and external training programs. Conducted over 100 Corporate,
Bank and Derivative Credit Risk week-long Seminars in 15 different countries.

1974-1994 JP MORGAN-
Credit Officer Global Markets '92-'94
Chairman, NACHO (North American Foreign Exchange Clearing House Organization)
Member, Executive Committee, ECHO (European Foreign Exchange Clearing House Organization)
Represented Global Markets' Credit in developing a single bank-wide credit system.
Rewrote and redesigned credit policy manual for bank-wide credit policy.
Designed and supervised implementation of computer tracking program for global sub-limits.
Credit Policy Department '83-'92
Chairman, North American Rating Committee -- rated all bank credit exposure.
Department Head, Risk Evaluation Group -- responsible for supervising 50 analysts.
Commercial Bank Management Program '82-'83
Administrator. Designed course content. Evaluated all trainees.
Financial Advisory Department '74-'82
Responsible for analytical work for internal ratings for manufacturing and basic industries.
Responsible for discontinuance of real estate lending in late 70's.

1967-1974 **SELF EMPLOYED**

1964-1967 **CITICORP – ASSISTANT BRANCH MANAGER**
Singapore, Kuala Lumpur

1959-1962 **U.S. NAVY – LTJG**
U.S. Naval Intelligence, Philippines

EDUCATION Masters Of Business Administration, Harvard University, 1964
1955-1964   achelor Of Arts, Williams College, 1959

PUBLICATIONS Co-authored **The Management of Racial Integration in Business** --
1964-2015   McGraw Hill 1964,
Authored **How to Avoid the Armageddon of 2054** -- Barringer Publishing 2015

Title: *Credit Analysis*
Author: Walter S. Foster
ISBN: 9781590959916

In credit analysis, we have three levels of certainty - facts we can know beyond all doubt, decisions we can make beyond a reasonable doubt and decisions we can make based upon the preponderance of evidence. For example, in legal analysis for civil cases, we only need to demonstrate our case by a preponderance of evidence. In legal analysis for criminal cases, we need to demonstrate our case beyond a reasonable doubt. In scientific proofs, we need to demonstrate our case beyond all doubt. In credit analysis some things we know beyond all doubt - for example accounting rules; some things we know beyond a reasonable doubt - for example financial statement analysis, and cash flow analysis; and finally some things we only know based upon the preponderance of evidence — for example credit analysis and credit understanding. Credit analysis is an art not a science, it comes up with probabilities for decision making under conditions of uncertainty.

This book clarifies this art from four perspectives – the perspective of the rating agencies, the perspective of the regulators, the perspective of the individual bank and the perspective of the derivative risk manager.

Rating agencies primarily attempt to evaluate the probability of default for individual bonds. There clients are investors who need help in evaluating the credit risk of their investors. Rating agencies evaluate of the business risk and financial risk of individual companies. Regulators primarily attempt to protect depositors from the default of the banking system. Their client is the US government which needs help in managing inflation and unemployment. Regulators evaluate the default risk of individual banks. Banks primarily attempt to evaluate the probability of loss for a portfolio of loans and financial activities. Their client is their shareholders who are looking for a return on their investment from dividends and appreciation in stock price. Banks attempt to evaluate the probability of default of their own bank. Derivative Risk Mangers primarily attempt to evaluate the probability of loss for their trading activities. Their client is the bank or investment bank senior management who are looking for a way to reduce their volatility of earnings.

Title: *How to Buy Bonds*
Author: Walter S. Foster
ISBN: 9781590959725

This book includes a half-hour of complimentary investment advice from the author.
This book shares with the unsophisticated investor criteria on how to evaluate bonds. The analysis is based on proper portfolio diversification and preservation of capital.

The greatest weakness of investors is that they panic in recessions and times of financial stress. As a result, they buy high and sell low. At the very time when investors should be increasing risk they have historically reduced it. And, at the very time when investors should be decreasing risk they have historically increased it. Studies have shown that the result is that market prices are about three times more volatile than they should be if one just evaluated the fundamentals.

The second greatest weakness of investors is that they pay high fees and buy and sell too often. Fees, commissions and spreads between the bid and ask price of stocks and bonds result in enormous drains on returns. Whether a stock or a bond fund, the normal fees for a small investor is 1% of assets and normal trading commissions are .5% of assets. Therefore, the total cost for an investment advisor is usually around 1.5%. Although the 1.5% may seem small relative to your total assets, it is 25% of your expected total annual return of about 6%.

The question is how to protect oneself from economic cycles and from one's own fears and ignorance. The answer is through a well understood principled and disciplined investment strategy. The objective of this book is to clarify an investment strategy for a mature investor with $100,000 to $2,000,000 to invest and the need to live off that investment. The objective of this book will be to recommend an investment strategy that requires that you only look at your investment portfolio once a year and make only one mathematical calculation to see if you need to adjust your monthly distributions from your investment portfolio. Another objective of this book is to recommend an investment strategy that forces you to sell high and buy low and reduce fees and trading commissions.

www.ingramcontent.com/pod-product-compliance
Lightning Source LLC
Chambersburg PA
CBHW042321090526
44585CB00024BA/2774